The Seed of the Sacred Fig Movie Review

Exploring Patriarchy and Visual Storytelling

Selena Davis

Copyright

All rights reserved. No part of this publication may be reproduced,
distributed, or transmitted in any form or by any means, including
photocopying, recording, or other electronic or mechanical methods,
without the prior written permission of the publisher, except in the case
of brief quotations embodied in critical reviews and certain other
noncommercial uses permitted by copyright law.
Copyright © (Selena Davis), (2024).

Table of Content

1. Introduction
Brief overview of the film
Director: Mohammad Rasoulof
Key themes: Iranian society, authoritarianism, patriarchy, and family dynamics
Context: Film's significance in Rasoulof's body of work and the political climate in Iran

2. Plot Summary
Synopsis of the film's storyline
Introduction to the main character: Iman
Key events and turning points in the narrative
Exploration of the family dynamics and external political conflict

3. Character Development and Performances
Iman (played by Missagh Zareh): A deeper look at his transformation and internal conflict
Najmeh (Soheila Golestani): Role in the family, her resilience, and response to the socio-political environment
The daughters, Rezvan and Sana: Their role in the narrative and generational differences with their father
Supporting characters: Impact on the story and their symbolic roles

4. Themes and Symbolism

Patriarchal violence and its implications
Theocracy and its moral consequences
The conflict between tradition and modernity
The symbolic significance of the gun and its metaphorical role in the narrative
Use of real-life protest footage and its relevance to the story

5. Cinematography and Visual Style
Rasoulof's direction and his distinctive visual style
Cinematographic techniques: Framing, lighting, and composition
The use of realism versus poetic symbolism in the visual narrative
Aesthetic contrasts in the rural setting versus the urban chaos

6. Soundtrack and Score
How music complements the emotional tone and tension
Use of silence and sound design to build atmosphere
The effect of the soundtrack on the film's pacing and intensity

7. Political Context and Social Commentary
Reflection of real-life Iranian protests and the oppression of women
Political subtext: Critique of the Iranian regime and authoritarian structures
The film's international relevance: How it speaks to global struggles for freedom and justice
Rasoulof's personal connection to the story and his real-life political exile

8. Pacing and Narrative Structure

The shift in tone from political drama to suspense thriller
The build-up of tension and how the film escalates
Handling of character development and thematic exploration within the structure
How the third act intensifies the emotional and political stakes

9. Criticism and Flaws
Examination of potential flaws in plot development or character arcs
Discussion on some of the film's ambiguities and missed opportunities
Possible disconnect between the narrative's realist elements and its more abstract moments

10. Conclusion
Overall assessment of the film
Evaluation of the performances, direction, and thematic execution
The film's significance within both Iranian cinema and world cinema
Final thoughts on its cultural relevance and political bravery

Introduction

The Seed of the Sacred Fig, directed by Mohammad Rasoulof, is a gripping political and family drama set in modern-day Iran. The film weaves together the personal and political as it explores themes of authoritarianism, societal repression, and the struggle for freedom. Set against the backdrop of widespread protests, the film focuses on Iman, a lawyer recently promoted to a state investigator role, his wife Najmeh, and their two daughters. At its core, The Seed of the Sacred Fig presents a story of moral dilemmas, familial discord, and the consequences of complicity in a corrupt regime.

The film's narrative begins with Iman's promotion to a higher-ranking position within the Revolutionary Court, where he is forced to reckon with the grim reality of Iran's judicial system. His job requires him to approve death sentences without reviewing the cases, pushing him into an ethical conflict that steadily unravels the moral fabric of his life. As Iman grapples with the pressures of his new role, the anti-hijab protests, inspired by real events, intensify, bringing his family into direct conflict with the repressive state apparatus he now represents. His daughters, particularly Rezvan, are drawn into the movement, further straining the father-daughter relationship. Tensions boil over when Iman's government-issued handgun goes missing, sparking a chain of events that ultimately leads to a volatile confrontation with his family. The film builds to a thrilling and emotionally charged climax, offering a poignant exploration of the personal costs of authoritarianism.

Director: Mohammad Rasoulof:

Mohammad Rasoulof, one of Iran's most prominent filmmakers, is known for his courageous body of work that often confronts the oppressive nature of the Iranian regime. Born in 1972, Rasoulof has faced considerable persecution for his outspoken criticism of the government. His films frequently explore themes of personal morality, state violence, and resistance. In many ways, The Seed of the Sacred Fig is a culmination of his previous works, which include There Is No Evil (2020), winner of the Golden Bear at the Berlin Film Festival, and Manuscripts Don't Burn (2013). Both films challenge the brutalities of state power in Iran, focusing on individuals who are forced to make impossible moral choices within oppressive systems.

Rasoulof's career has been marked by a constant tension between his artistic vision and the constraints imposed by the Iranian authorities. His films have often been banned in Iran, and he has faced repeated arrests, prison sentences, and travel bans. In fact, The Seed of the Sacred Fig was made under extreme circumstances, with the filmmaker fleeing arrest during its production and the film being edited in exile. Rasoulof's work is not only a reflection of the realities of life in Iran but also a personal testament to the sacrifices artists make in the name of truth and justice.

Key Themes: Iranian Society, Authoritarianism, Patriarchy, and Family Dynamics:

The Seed of the Sacred Fig delves deeply into the intersection of political repression and family life in Iran. The film is set during a time of intense political upheaval, inspired by the real-life protests that erupted following the death of 22-year-old Jina Mahsa Amini, who died in police custody after being arrested for not properly wearing her hijab. This tragedy ignited widespread protests, particularly among women, against the oppressive rules enforced by the Islamic Republic's morality police. The film's portrayal of these protests brings the harsh realities of Iranian society into sharp focus, highlighting the courage of women and youth who defy the government's draconian rules.

One of the central themes of the film is authoritarianism and the way it permeates both the public and private spheres of life. Iman's role as a state investigator symbolizes the corrupt and violent nature of Iran's judicial system. His job forces him to sign off on death penalties without due process, underscoring how theocratic authority exerts its will on the individual, stripping people of their autonomy and humanity. This authoritarianism seeps into Iman's personal life, poisoning his relationships with his wife and daughters. The film deftly portrays the psychological toll of living under constant state surveillance, where even within families, trust erodes, and paranoia reigns.

The theme of patriarchy is also central to the film. Iman, as the patriarch of his family, becomes a metaphor for the larger system of male dominance in Iran. His relationship with his daughters, particularly Rezvan, is marked by a sense of ownership and control. Iman's belief that he knows best for his family reflects the broader societal expectations placed on women to be obedient and subservient. The film's exploration of this dynamic reaches a boiling point when Iman's gun goes missing, leading to a tense standoff in which the women of the family assert their own agency against his tyrannical control. The gun, a symbol of male power and violence, becomes a focal point for the film's critique of patriarchal authority.

Family dynamics are at the heart of The Seed of the Sacred Fig, as the film explores how the personal is political. Najmeh, Iman's wife, serves as the mediator between her husband's oppressive role and their daughters' defiance. The generational conflict between Iman and his daughters reflects the broader societal divide between conservative and progressive forces in Iran. The daughters represent a new generation that refuses to be silenced, their participation in the protests mirroring the real-life bravery of Iran's youth. This clash of values within the family mirrors the larger societal struggle, with the home becoming a microcosm of the nation's political conflict.

Context: Film's Significance in Rasoulof's Body of Work and the Political Climate in Iran:

The Seed of the Sacred Fig is a significant entry in Rasoulof's oeuvre, continuing his commitment to exposing the injustices of the Iranian regime. Like his previous films, it critiques the mechanisms of power that maintain the Islamic Republic's authoritarian rule, while also offering a deeply personal story about the human cost of complicity in such a regime. The film's integration of real-life protest footage adds a layer of urgency and immediacy, blurring the lines between fiction and documentary. By doing so, Rasoulof bridges the gap between art and activism, using cinema as a tool for resistance.

The political climate in Iran, particularly in the aftermath of the 2022 protests, provides the backdrop for The Seed of the Sacred Fig. The film is not just a reflection of the past but a commentary on the present, offering a powerful indictment of the government's ongoing repression of dissent. In a country where filmmakers are routinely silenced, Rasoulof's decision to smuggle footage and complete the film despite immense personal risk is an act of defiance. The Seed of the Sacred Fig is both a cry for justice and a testament to the resilience of those who continue to fight for freedom, even in the face of overwhelming oppression.

Through this film, Rasoulof not only challenges the status quo in Iran but also speaks to a global audience about the dangers of authoritarianism, the importance of dissent, and the enduring power of cinema to inspire change.

Chapter 2.

Plot Summary

The Seed of the Sacred Fig tells the story of Iman, a lawyer and family man whose recent promotion to a state investigator in Iran's Revolutionary Court brings him face to face with the moral and political complexities of his country. The film opens with Iman receiving this new post, which grants him better pay, improved living conditions for his family, and greater status in society. However, what at first seems like a prestigious career opportunity quickly becomes a burden, as Iman is confronted with the grim realities of his work. His role requires him to approve death penalty sentences without reviewing the evidence an authoritarian process that reveals the corrupt and dehumanizing nature of the judicial system.

As Iman grapples with his new responsibilities, the political climate in Iran begins to shift. Protests, particularly those led by women resisting the country's mandatory hijab laws, break out across the nation. These protests are inspired by real-life events, including the death of Mahsa Amini, which sparked a nationwide movement against the theocratic regime's treatment of women. The film uses this historical moment to depict the broader struggle for freedom in Iran and the ways in which it impacts the personal lives of ordinary citizens like Iman and his family.

Introduction to the Main Character: Iman:

Iman, portrayed by Missagh Zareh, is a complex and morally conflicted character. At the start of the film, he is presented as a conscientious and somewhat naive man who believes in the rule of law and sees his new position as an opportunity to better provide for his family. Iman is a devoted husband to Najmeh (Soheila Golestani) and a father to two daughters, Rezvan (Setareh Malek) and Giti (Mahsa Rostami), both of whom are in their early twenties and attending university. While Iman seems to care deeply for his family, there is an undercurrent of tension in his relationships, particularly with his daughters, whose views on Iran's political and social situation are far more liberal than his own.

As Iman's work exposes him to the darker side of the legal system, his character undergoes a transformation. He is forced to confront the reality that his job is not about justice but about enforcing the will of the state, often at the cost of human life. This internal conflict causes Iman to retreat emotionally from his family, becoming increasingly paranoid and authoritarian in his own home. The film masterfully portrays Iman's gradual descent into moral ambiguity, as he wrestles with his conscience while trying to maintain the appearance of control.

Key Events and Turning Points in the Narrative:

One of the first major turning points in the film occurs when Iman is assigned his first case involving the death penalty. His superior instructs him to approve the sentence without reading the file, a clear violation of due process. At this moment, Iman realizes that his role in the system is not to deliver justice, but to rubber-stamp the regime's decisions. This revelation deeply unsettles him, but he initially tries to rationalize his complicity, believing that his family's security and well-being depend on his continued loyalty to the state.

The second key event in the film is the escalation of the anti-hijab protests. These protests serve as a catalyst for much of the personal and political tension in the story. Iman's daughters, especially Rezvan, are sympathetic to the protesters and quietly express their support for the movement. Rezvan, in particular, becomes more vocal about her opposition to the regime's oppressive policies, leading to arguments with her father. Iman, who now sees himself as part of the state apparatus, views his daughters' dissent as not only dangerous but also a personal betrayal. He becomes increasingly authoritarian in his household, attempting to impose the same kind of control over his family that he enforces at work.

The disappearance of Iman's government-issued handgun marks a pivotal turning point in the narrative. After being given the gun for his family's protection, Iman neglects to properly secure it, leaving it lying around the house. When the gun goes missing, he immediately suspects one of the women in his family of taking it. This event amplifies the existing tensions between Iman and his family, leading him to become even more paranoid and distrustful. He confronts his wife and daughters, accusing them of undermining his authority and potentially aiding the anti-government protesters. The missing gun becomes a symbol of Iman's lost control both in his household and in his professional life and serves as the film's central plot device, driving the action forward toward its explosive conclusion.

Exploration of the Family Dynamics and External Political Conflict:

The dynamics within Iman's family are crucial to understanding the broader political conflict that the film portrays. Iman represents the older generation of Iranians who have either resigned themselves to the regime's power or have found ways to justify their complicity. In contrast, his daughters symbolize the younger generation, who are fed up with the repression and are willing to take risks in order to challenge the status quo. This generational divide is evident in the conversations Iman has with his daughters, particularly Rezvan, who becomes increasingly defiant as the film progresses.

Najmeh, Iman's wife, plays a more passive role in the family dynamic, but she is not without agency. While she does not openly defy her husband, she is sympathetic to her daughters' views and quietly supports their resistance to his increasingly dictatorial behavior. Najmeh's role as mediator between Iman and the daughters reflects the position of many women in Iranian society who, while not at the forefront of political movements, are deeply affected by the country's oppressive policies and contribute to the struggle for change in subtle but significant ways.

As the external political conflict intensifies, so too does the internal conflict within Iman's household. The protests, which begin as background noise in the film's early scenes, soon take center stage as the government's violent crackdown escalates. The family's involvement in the protests becomes inevitable when Najmeh and the daughters offer refuge to a young woman who has been injured during a demonstration. This act of defiance brings the external political conflict directly into the family's home, setting up the final confrontation between Iman and his family.

The film's climax is both emotionally and politically charged. Iman, desperate to regain control and protect his status, becomes increasingly erratic in his behavior. The missing gun, now a symbol of his unraveling authority, reappears in a shocking and violent way, forcing Iman to confront the consequences of his actions. The final moments of the film leave the audience with a sense of both tragedy and hope, as the personal and political collide in a powerful statement about the cost of authoritarianism and the possibility of resistance.

Through its exploration of family dynamics and the external political conflict, The Seed of the Sacred Fig offers a nuanced and deeply human portrayal of life under an oppressive regime. The film does not shy away from depicting the harsh realities of authoritarianism, but it also highlights the resilience and courage of those who resist, even in the face of overwhelming odds. As Iman's story unfolds, it becomes clear that the struggle for freedom is not only a political battle but also a deeply personal one, fought within the walls of the family home.

Chapter 3.

Character Development and Performances

In The Seed of the Sacred Fig, character development serves as the emotional and thematic backbone of the film. Each member of Iman's family is intricately woven into the larger narrative, representing different facets of Iranian society and embodying the internal struggles that arise under oppressive regimes. The performances are compelling and provide depth to the characters' psychological and emotional journeys, particularly in the context of political and social repression. This chapter will explore the development of the central characters, focusing on how their roles contribute to the film's overarching themes of power, control, resistance, and familial loyalty.

Iman (Missagh Zareh): A Deeper Look at His Transformation and Internal Conflict:

At the heart of the film is Iman, played by Missagh Zareh, whose journey from an upright, idealistic lawyer to a morally conflicted and increasingly authoritarian figure is the central arc of The Seed of the Sacred Fig. Iman's transformation is gradual but deeply significant, mirroring the erosion of individual agency in the face of oppressive state systems. Zareh's performance is understated yet powerful, capturing the internal conflict that defines his character's downward spiral.

At the outset, Iman appears as a man of principle, proud of his new position as a state investigator, which offers financial stability and elevated social standing for his family. His initial excitement is evident, and Zareh portrays this early version of Iman with a sense of hopefulness, believing that his new role will bring positive changes to his life. However, this hope is quickly shattered when Iman realizes that his position is not about administering justice, but rather about enforcing the will of a regime that devalues human life. His disillusionment begins when he is instructed to rubber-stamp death penalty judgments without reviewing the cases, and from this moment on, we witness Iman's moral descent.

Zareh expertly conveys Iman's internal conflict as he struggles to reconcile his duty to the state with his own moral compass. Iman's transformation is not just external but deeply psychological. The demands of his job pull him further away from his family, and his increasing paranoia highlighted by the missing gun leads him to project his internal frustrations onto them. This paranoia is symptomatic of a larger fear of losing control, not only over his work but also over his personal life. The film suggests that the pressures of living under authoritarian rule often manifest in the microcosm of the family, where power dynamics become distorted and harmful. Iman's journey, then, is one of disillusionment and alienation, and Zareh captures this arc with a performance that oscillates between vulnerability and coldness.

As Iman becomes more authoritarian in his own home, he loses the ability to empathize with his daughters, Rezvan and Giti, who challenge his worldview. The family tension climaxes when Iman accuses one of them of stealing his gun, which has gone missing—a symbol of both his professional and personal impotence. His transformation is complete when he becomes consumed by rage and suspicion, losing the moral clarity that initially defined him. By the film's end, Iman is a tragic figure, emblematic of those who, in seeking to protect their loved ones, become complicit in the very systems they once opposed.

Najmeh (Soheila Golestani):

Role in the Family, Her Resilience, and Response to the Socio-Political Environment

Najmeh, played by Soheila Golestani, is the quiet but resolute pillar of the family. While much of the film centers on Iman's internal conflict, Najmeh's role as the emotional anchor of the household is equally important. Golestani's performance is nuanced, showing a woman who must navigate the tightrope between supporting her husband and shielding her daughters from his growing authoritarian tendencies. Najmeh's character embodies the experience of many women in Iran caught between oppressive societal expectations and the desire to protect their families from harm.

Early in the film, Najmeh appears as a dutiful wife, supportive of Iman's new job and proud of the financial stability it brings to the family. However, as Iman becomes more withdrawn and authoritarian, Najmeh's role shifts from passive support to active resistance, albeit in subtle ways. She begins to quietly side with her daughters, particularly when it comes to the socio-political issues that divide the family. While she never openly confronts Iman, Golestani conveys Najmeh's internal struggle through small acts of defiance such as when she helps shelter a wounded anti-hijab protester, despite knowing the risk it poses to her family.

Najmeh's resilience is central to the film's exploration of familial loyalty and resistance. She understands the danger that her husband's job represents, not just to his morality but to the safety of their family, yet she continues to fulfill her role as mediator between Iman and their daughters. Her subtle resistance to Iman's increasingly autocratic behavior reflects the quiet defiance of many Iranian women, who find ways to subvert patriarchal control while navigating the constraints of their social roles. Golestani's performance gives Najmeh a quiet strength that is crucial to the film's emotional core, and her character provides a counterbalance to Iman's authoritarianism, representing the possibility of compassion and understanding in a repressive environment.

The Daughters, Rezvan and Giti:

Their Role in the Narrative and Generational Differences with Their Father

Rezvan and Giti, Iman's daughters, represent the generational shift in Iran, with the younger generation rejecting the state's oppressive policies and seeking greater freedom. Rezvan, the older of the two, played by Setareh Malek, is particularly outspoken in her defiance of her father's authority and the regime he represents. Giti, played by Mahsa Rostami, is quieter but equally affected by the political climate, and together, the sisters challenge their father's worldview.

The daughters' relationship with Iman is central to the film's exploration of generational conflict. While Iman clings to the belief that loyalty to the state will ensure his family's security, Rezvan and Giti see the regime for what it is an oppressive force that seeks to control their bodies and minds. Rezvan, in particular, serves as the voice of the younger generation, questioning her father's complicity and pushing back against his attempts to silence her. In one particularly powerful scene, Rezvan confronts Iman over his support for the government's policies, accusing him of betraying the very values he once claimed to uphold.

The generational divide between Iman and his daughters is not just about politics, but also about identity. Rezvan and Giti have grown up in a world where access to information through social media has exposed them to alternative perspectives, making them more aware of the injustices their father seeks to deny. Their defiance is a key turning point in the film, as it forces Iman to confront the reality that his daughters do not share his worldview, and that their loyalty to him is not unconditional.

Supporting Characters: Impact on the Story and Their Symbolic Roles

The supporting characters in The Seed of the Sacred Fig serve symbolic roles that enhance the film's exploration of power, control, and resistance. One of the most significant is the young female protester whom Najmeh and the daughters shelter after she is injured during an anti-hijab demonstration. This character, though unnamed, represents the broader movement for women's rights in Iran and the personal stakes of the political struggle. Her presence in the family's home brings the external conflict into their domestic sphere, forcing Iman to confront the consequences of his complicity in the regime's violence.

Another important supporting character is Iman's superior in the judiciary, who serves as the embodiment of the state's authoritarian power. His interactions with Iman highlight the dehumanizing nature of the regime, as he dismisses Iman's moral concerns and reinforces the idea that loyalty to the state is more important than justice. This character is a chilling reminder of the systemic corruption that permeates every level of the judiciary, and his cold, bureaucratic demeanor contrasts sharply with Iman's early idealism.

Together, these supporting characters enhance the film's themes of power and resistance, providing the external pressures that drive the central family's internal conflict. They serve as symbols of the broader socio-political forces at play, while also contributing to the personal stakes of the narrative.

Chapter 4.

Themes and Symbolism

In The Seed of the Sacred Fig, Mohammad Rasoulof skillfully interweaves various themes that reflect the complex socio-political landscape of Iran. The film delves deep into the intersections of personal and political spheres, offering a rich tapestry of symbolism that underscores the internal and external conflicts faced by the characters. The dominant themes of patriarchal violence, theocracy, the clash between tradition and modernity, and the metaphorical role of the gun all contribute to a narrative that is as much about individual struggle as it is about systemic oppression. Additionally, the incorporation of real-life protest footage heightens the film's immediacy, anchoring its story in the ongoing fight for freedom in Iran.

Patriarchal Violence and Its Implications:

Patriarchal violence is a central theme in The Seed of the Sacred Fig, shaping the dynamics within Iman's family and reflecting the broader authoritarian structures of Iranian society. Iman, who begins the film as a loving father and husband, gradually succumbs to the pressures of the patriarchal state, adopting its methods of control and oppression in his own home. The violence of the patriarchal system is not always physical; often, it manifests as a psychological force, exerting control over women's autonomy and freedom. In this sense, Iman's character transformation can be viewed as a microcosm of how authoritarian regimes enforce patriarchal norms through coercion and intimidation.

Iman's increasing authoritarianism mirrors the state's systematic violence against women. As a father and husband, he is expected to maintain control over his household, and as his professional role as a state investigator puts him in closer proximity to the regime's methods, his behavior becomes more controlling and violent. This patriarchal violence becomes most apparent in his interactions with his daughters, Rezvan and Giti, as they challenge his authority. Iman's attempts to stifle their voices reflect the state's broader attempts to suppress dissent, particularly from women who demand more autonomy and freedom. The film critiques the way in which patriarchal systems, supported by the state, permeate even the most intimate of family spaces, corrupting the relationships between loved ones.

Najmeh, Iman's wife, and the daughters are forced to navigate the violence imposed by Iman, but they do so in different ways. Najmeh employs quiet resistance, finding subtle ways to oppose Iman's control, while the daughters are more vocal and direct in their defiance. Through their resistance, the film critiques the patriarchal expectation that women should be obedient and compliant. Instead, the women in the film are portrayed as resilient and courageous, even in the face of overwhelming power. This resistance is not only against Iman but also against the larger system that he represents. The film's portrayal of patriarchal violence and its consequences emphasizes the suffocating environment women endure and the emotional toll it takes on family life.

Theocracy and Its Moral Consequences:

The theme of theocracy is intricately connected to the film's exploration of moral decay and the consequences of blind adherence to authoritarian systems. Iran's theocratic regime, with its strict interpretation of Islamic law, exerts enormous influence over the lives of its citizens, particularly through the judicial system, where Iman is employed. The film illustrates how theocratic rule distorts moral values, transforming those in positions of authority, like Iman, into enforcers of unjust and often violent laws.

Iman's disillusionment with his role in the judiciary is central to the film's critique of theocracy. Initially, he believes that his new position as a state investigator will allow him to serve justice, but he quickly learns that his role is not about morality or fairness. Instead, he is expected to rubber-stamp death sentences without reviewing the evidence, a task that contradicts his personal sense of justice. This realization triggers Iman's moral decline, as he begins to internalize the theocratic regime's values, prioritizing loyalty to the state over his own moral principles.

The film suggests that theocracy corrupts not only individuals but entire social systems, breeding a culture of fear, mistrust, and moral ambiguity. Iman's transformation into a morally compromised figure highlights the dangers of allowing religious doctrine to dictate law and governance. The theocratic system strips individuals of their agency and moral responsibility, reducing them to mere cogs in a machine that perpetuates violence and oppression. The film's portrayal of theocracy is thus a sharp critique of the ways in which religious authority can be weaponized to enforce conformity and suppress dissent, with devastating moral consequences.

The Conflict Between Tradition and Modernity:

The Seed of the Sacred Fig also explores the tension between tradition and modernity, a theme that is particularly relevant in the context of contemporary Iranian society. This conflict is most evident in the generational divide between Iman and his daughters. While Iman clings to traditional values and the authority of the state, Rezvan and Giti represent a younger generation that is more attuned to modern, globalized ideas of freedom, equality, and individualism.

Iman's adherence to traditional values is largely shaped by his desire for stability and control, both within his family and in his professional life. He believes that by aligning himself with the state and its traditionalist, theocratic values, he can protect his family and maintain order. However, this belief is challenged by his daughters, who reject the state's control over their bodies and minds. The conflict between Iman and his daughters represents the broader struggle in Iranian society between those who seek to preserve traditional, patriarchal norms and those who advocate for progressive change.

The film's portrayal of this generational conflict underscores the challenges that arise when tradition is used as a tool of control rather than a source of cultural identity. While Iman views tradition as a means of maintaining social order, his daughters see it as an oppressive force that stifles their freedom. The tension between tradition and modernity is thus central to the film's exploration of familial and societal conflict, with each generation representing different responses to the changing political and cultural landscape of Iran.

The Symbolic Significance of the Gun and Its Metaphorical Role in the Narrative:

The gun in The Seed of the Sacred Fig serves as one of the film's most potent symbols, representing power, control, and the moral corruption that comes with authoritarianism. Introduced early in the narrative when Iman is issued the gun for his family's protection, it quickly becomes a metaphor for the destructive force of state-sanctioned violence. Iman's casual attitude toward the gun, leaving it lying around the house, reflects his naiveté about the dangers of power and the ease with which violence can infiltrate the domestic sphere.

As the film progresses, the missing gun becomes a source of paranoia and distrust within the family, symbolizing the breakdown of familial bonds under the weight of authoritarian control. Iman's suspicion that one of his daughters has taken the gun reflects his growing fear of losing control, both over his family and over his own sense of morality. The gun, therefore, becomes a symbol of Iman's internal conflict, as well as the larger societal struggle between freedom and control.

The Chekhovian principle that a gun introduced in the first act must be used by the third is fulfilled in the film's climax, where the gun's presence takes on even greater symbolic significance. Its eventual use underscores the destructive consequences of Iman's moral compromise and the broader violence of the regime he serves. The gun, as a metaphor, encapsulates the film's central themes of power, control, and the moral decay that accompanies the acceptance of authoritarianism.

Use of Real-Life Protest Footage and Its Relevance to the Story:

The inclusion of real-life protest footage in The Seed of the Sacred Fig grounds the film in the contemporary political reality of Iran, where protests against the regime's oppressive policies, particularly those targeting women, have been widespread. This footage, interwoven with the fictional narrative, serves as a powerful reminder that the struggles depicted in the film are not merely allegorical but are reflective of real events and real people fighting for their rights.

The use of this footage adds a layer of urgency to the film, connecting the personal struggles of Iman's family with the broader socio-political unrest in Iran. The protests, particularly those led by women against the compulsory hijab laws, resonate with the film's themes of resistance and defiance. By incorporating this footage, Rasoulof situates the film within the larger movement for change in Iran, making the characters' personal struggles emblematic of the country's fight for freedom and justice.

In conclusion, The Seed of the Sacred Fig is a rich, multilayered film that uses symbolism and thematic depth to explore the personal and political consequences of authoritarianism. Through its exploration of patriarchal violence, theocracy, the conflict between tradition and modernity, and the symbolic use of the gun, the film offers a powerful critique of power and control in contemporary Iranian society. The incorporation of real-life protest footage further enhances its relevance, grounding the narrative in the ongoing fight for freedom in Iran.

Chapter 5.

Cinematography and Visual Style

In The Seed of the Sacred Fig, Mohammad Rasoulof's distinctive visual style plays a pivotal role in conveying the emotional and thematic weight of the film. As a director known for his defiant approach to politically charged narratives, Rasoulof's mastery of cinematography reflects the personal and societal struggles central to the story. The film's visual narrative oscillates between realism and poetic symbolism, using framing, lighting, and composition to deepen the audience's engagement with the complex themes of authoritarianism, patriarchy, and individual freedom. The visual contrasts between rural and urban settings further underscore the tension between tradition and modernity, creating a striking aesthetic that mirrors the internal conflict of the characters.

Rasoulof's Direction and His Distinctive Visual Style:

Rasoulof's direction is marked by his ability to merge a grounded, realistic portrayal of life under authoritarianism with an almost surreal use of symbolism and metaphor. In The Seed of the Sacred Fig, his visual style captures the oppressive atmosphere of Iranian society, while also allowing moments of visual poetry that elevate the film's emotional and thematic complexity. As a dissident filmmaker working under constant threat of persecution, Rasoulof's direction is both a form of artistic resistance and a deeply personal expression of defiance.

One of Rasoulof's key strengths as a director is his ability to create tension through visual storytelling. Rather than relying on dialogue to convey the inner lives of his characters, Rasoulof often uses visual cues such as lingering shots of empty spaces, or the positioning of characters within the frame to communicate their emotional states. For example, Iman's growing isolation and paranoia are reflected in the way he is often framed in confined spaces, with the camera trapping him in tight, claustrophobic shots. This visual representation of Iman's internal conflict mirrors his increasing alienation from his family and his own moral compass, heightening the film's sense of emotional and psychological claustrophobia.

Rasoulof's use of long takes and minimal camera movement also contributes to the film's sense of realism, allowing the audience to fully immerse themselves in the world of the characters. These long, unbroken shots give the viewer time to absorb the tension building within the scenes, creating a sense of inevitability and dread. This stylistic choice reflects Rasoulof's commitment to a kind of visual honesty, where the camera becomes a silent observer of the unfolding drama, rather than an active participant.

Cinematographic Techniques: Framing, Lighting, and Composition:

Framing plays a crucial role in The Seed of the Sacred Fig, particularly in how Rasoulof uses the camera to emphasize power dynamics and emotional distance between characters. Iman, for instance, is often framed separately from his family, even when they share the same space. This separation visually underscores the growing emotional rift between him and his wife and daughters as he becomes more entrenched in his role as a state investigator. By physically isolating Iman within the frame, Rasoulof visually reinforces the idea that his alignment with the regime has cut him off from his family's shared values and sense of solidarity.

Lighting in the film is used not only to set the mood but also to symbolically reflect the moral and psychological states of the characters. The film often employs stark, naturalistic lighting, particularly in scenes where the family is shown in their home. The harsh, unfiltered light in these scenes contrasts with the darker, more shadowed lighting used in Iman's workplace, where his moral compromises take shape. This contrast between light and dark serves as a visual metaphor for the moral clarity that Iman abandons as he succumbs to the pressures of his new role. In key moments, such as the discovery of the missing gun, Rasoulof shifts to more dramatic lighting, using shadows to create a sense of unease and tension, visually representing the creeping sense of danger that threatens to engulf the family.

Composition is another essential tool that Rasoulof uses to communicate themes of control and rebellion. Characters are often positioned in ways that reflect their social roles and the power dynamics at play. For instance, in scenes where Iman confronts his daughters, the composition frequently places him in the foreground, towering over them, while they are seated or framed in a more vulnerable position. This visual arrangement not only highlights the patriarchal authority he exerts over his family but also foreshadows the rebellion that his daughters will eventually wage against him. The film's composition thus becomes a visual representation of the struggle for power and autonomy within the family, mirroring the broader societal struggle against authoritarian rule.

The Use of Realism Versus Poetic Symbolism in the Visual Narrative:

One of the defining features of The Seed of the Sacred Fig is its fluid transition between realism and poetic symbolism. Rasoulof's use of realism is most evident in his depiction of the mundane aspects of the characters' lives the everyday conversations, the routine movements around the house, and the quiet moments of family interaction. This realism grounds the film in a recognizable world, making the characters' emotional and political struggles feel immediate and relatable.

However, Rasoulof also uses moments of poetic symbolism to elevate the narrative beyond the confines of realism, allowing the film to engage with broader philosophical and political questions. The gun, as a recurring visual motif, is one of the most powerful examples of this symbolism. Throughout the film, the gun functions not just as a physical object, but as a metaphor for the violence and control that permeates both the family and the state. Its presence looms over the characters, even when it is not visible on screen, representing the ever-present threat of authoritarian power and the consequences of moral compromise.

Another symbolic element is the recurring motif of doors and thresholds, which appear frequently in the film as visual representations of boundaries—both physical and emotional. Doors are often shown closing or being locked, symbolizing the barriers that Iman erects between himself and his family. These thresholds also represent the liminal spaces that the characters occupy, caught between the demands of tradition and the desire for modernity and freedom. The symbolism of crossing thresholds becomes particularly poignant in scenes where the daughters attempt to escape their father's control, suggesting a metaphorical crossing into a new realm of independence and self-determination.

Aesthetic Contrasts in the Rural Setting Versus the Urban Chaos:

The visual contrasts between the film's rural and urban settings serve as a metaphor for the larger conflict between tradition and modernity that runs through the narrative. The rural setting, where the family resides, is depicted with a sense of calm and stillness, characterized by wide-open spaces and natural light. This setting represents the traditional values that Iman holds onto, as well as the illusion of control and stability that he tries to maintain in his personal life. The rural landscape, with its quiet beauty and isolation, contrasts sharply with the chaos of the urban environment, where political unrest and violence are omnipresent.

In contrast, the scenes set in the city are marked by frenetic energy and disorienting camera movements, reflecting the chaos and instability of the political climate. The urban setting is often shown through fragmented, handheld shots that capture the protests and unrest in a visceral, almost documentary-like style. The visual chaos of the city mirrors the internal turmoil of the characters, particularly Iman, who is increasingly torn between his loyalty to the state and his responsibility to his family. This aesthetic contrast between the rural and urban settings reinforces the film's exploration of the conflict between the desire for personal freedom and the oppressive forces of tradition and authoritarianism.

The city, with its noise, movement, and unpredictability, represents the forces of change that threaten to upend the traditional order that Iman clings to. In contrast, the rural home is depicted as a space of retreat and safety, but one that ultimately proves to be an illusion, as the violence of the outside world inevitably penetrates its walls. This visual dichotomy between the rural and urban settings highlights the characters' struggle to reconcile their personal desires with the larger socio-political forces that shape their lives.

Conclusion:

Rasoulof's direction and visual style in The Seed of the Sacred Fig are integral to the film's emotional and thematic depth. Through careful attention to framing, lighting, and composition, Rasoulof crafts a visual narrative that reflects the internal and external conflicts faced by the characters. The film's use of realism, interspersed with moments of poetic symbolism, creates a rich and layered viewing experience, while the visual contrasts between rural and urban settings reinforce the film's exploration of tradition, modernity, and authoritarianism. In Rasoulof's hands, cinematography becomes not just a tool for storytelling but a means of articulating the complex power dynamics and moral struggles at the heart of the film.

Chapter 6.

Soundtrack and Score

The soundtrack and score of The Seed of the Sacred Fig play an essential role in shaping the emotional landscape and tension throughout the film. Mohammad Rasoulof, known for his careful attention to detail, uses music and sound to complement the narrative's complex themes of familial conflict, authoritarianism, and personal moral struggle. The interplay between music, silence, and carefully crafted sound design helps establish the mood, enhances key moments of tension, and supports the overall pacing of the film. In The Seed of the Sacred Fig, music is not just an accessory but a powerful narrative device that deepens the viewer's connection to the story.

How Music Complements the Emotional Tone and Tension:

From the opening sequence to the final moments, the music in The Seed of the Sacred Fig acts as an emotional guide for the audience, shaping their perception of the film's tone and heightening the emotional impact of key scenes. Rasoulof's film, which deals with intense themes like authoritarian control, domestic strife, and moral decay, often uses music to reflect the underlying emotional states of the characters.

The score is subtle, yet powerful, leaning on minimalist compositions that create a haunting, introspective atmosphere. Rather than overpowering the narrative, the music in this film often operates in the background, like a pulse that gradually builds, mirroring the growing tension within Iman's family and the broader political environment. For example, during scenes where Iman struggles with his conscience or confronts his family, the music gently underscores his internal conflict, using slow, repetitive melodies that emphasize the weight of his choices.

In more intense moments, such as when Iman's gun goes missing or during the climactic confrontation between him and his family, the score shifts to a darker, more urgent tone. The music becomes more dissonant, employing strings and percussive elements that evoke a sense of dread and uncertainty. This shift in the score not only enhances the emotional stakes of the scene but also reflects Iman's spiraling psychological state, as he loses control of both his family and his sense of moral clarity.

The use of traditional Iranian musical motifs is also present in the film, adding a layer of cultural depth to the score. These motifs, which may be unfamiliar to some viewers, resonate with the themes of tradition and modernity that are central to the film's narrative. By incorporating these elements into the score, Rasoulof reinforces the tension between the old and the new, the past and the present, that permeates the lives of the characters.

Use of Silence and Sound Design to Build Atmosphere:

Equally important to the soundtrack of The Seed of the Sacred Fig is the deliberate use of silence and sound design. Silence, in particular, is used as a powerful narrative tool to emphasize the emotional isolation of the characters, especially Iman. Rasoulof employs silence not just in moments of reflection but also to heighten tension and anticipation, allowing the viewer to feel the weight of the unspoken words and the unresolved conflicts that simmer beneath the surface.

For example, in scenes where Iman interacts with his daughters, particularly after the anti-hijab protests have escalated, Rasoulof often chooses to let the dialogue fade into silence, leaving only the ambient sounds of the household the clink of cutlery, the rustle of clothes, or the creak of a chair. This silence creates a palpable sense of discomfort, as the audience is left to absorb the emotional distance between Iman and his family. It's a deliberate choice that forces the viewer to confront the oppressive atmosphere in the household, as well as Iman's increasing alienation from those he loves.

Sound design plays an equally significant role in building the film's atmosphere. Rasoulof's attention to auditory detail is evident in his use of everyday sounds to reflect the psychological state of the characters. The quiet hum of city life, the distant sounds of protests, and the subtle creaking of floorboards in the family home are all used to create an immersive soundscape that mirrors the emotional tension within the film. The sound of Iman's gun being handled, for instance, is amplified in key moments, creating a visceral connection between the object and the threat it represents. The sharp, metallic click of the gun's safety being turned off or the faint rustle of fabric as Iman tucks it into his waistband serve as auditory reminders of the violence that lurks just beneath the surface of the family's interactions.

The absence of music in certain scenes also plays a crucial role in building tension. By stripping away the score and relying solely on ambient sounds or silence, Rasoulof creates an eerie, suspenseful atmosphere that heightens the emotional stakes of the narrative. One notable example is the scene where Iman discovers that his gun is missing. Instead of using music to signal the importance of the moment, Rasoulof opts for silence, allowing the viewer to feel the full weight of Iman's panic and confusion. The silence amplifies the sense of dread, as Iman frantically searches for the weapon, and the tension is allowed to build naturally without the intrusion of a musical cue.

The Effect of the Soundtrack on the Film's Pacing and Intensity:

The soundtrack of The Seed of the Sacred Fig is carefully designed to complement the film's pacing, which fluctuates between slow, introspective moments and bursts of intense action. Rasoulof uses music to control the rhythm of the film, slowing it down during reflective scenes and ramping up the intensity during moments of conflict. This dynamic use of the score helps maintain a sense of balance in the film's pacing, ensuring that the narrative never feels rushed or disjointed.

In the quieter, more contemplative scenes, the music is minimalistic and slow, allowing the audience to fully absorb the emotional nuances of the characters' interactions. This slower pace mirrors the internal struggles of the characters, particularly Iman, whose journey is marked by a gradual unraveling of his moral certainty. The music in these scenes acts almost like a metronome, keeping time with Iman's internal deliberations as he grapples with the ethical compromises required by his new role as a state investigator.

Conversely, during the more intense sequences such as the climactic confrontation between Iman and his family, or the car chase that occurs later in the film the music shifts to a faster, more urgent tempo. The score becomes louder, more discordant, reflecting the chaos and violence that have erupted in the narrative. These moments of heightened intensity are underscored by a driving rhythm that propels the action forward, increasing the viewer's sense of anxiety and anticipation. The music works in tandem with the visual elements of the film to create a visceral, immersive experience that draws the audience into the emotional core of the story.

The soundtrack also plays a crucial role in shaping the film's emotional peaks and valleys. By carefully modulating the music's intensity, Rasoulof is able to create moments of release after periods of sustained tension. For example, after a particularly intense confrontation between Iman and his daughters, the music shifts to a softer, more melancholic tone, allowing the audience to momentarily relax before the tension begins to build again. This ebb and flow of musical intensity helps maintain the film's dramatic tension without overwhelming the viewer.

In some scenes, the music completely disappears, leaving only the ambient sounds of the environment to fill the space. This absence of music serves to heighten the emotional impact of certain moments, as the viewer is forced to confront the raw, unfiltered emotions of the characters without the buffer of a musical score. The decision to withhold music in these key scenes is a testament to Rasoulof's confidence in his actors' performances and his belief in the power of silence to convey meaning.

Conclusion:

The soundtrack and score of The Seed of the Sacred Fig are integral to the film's overall impact, shaping its emotional tone, pacing, and intensity. Through the careful use of music, silence, and sound design, Rasoulof creates a rich auditory landscape that complements the film's visual storytelling. The music not only enhances the emotional depth of the characters' journeys but also reflects the broader political and social tensions that drive the narrative. By balancing moments of silence with carefully composed musical cues, Rasoulof is able to build a sense of atmosphere and tension that keeps the audience engaged from beginning to end. Ultimately, the soundtrack serves as a powerful narrative tool, deepening the viewer's connection to the film's themes and characters while amplifying the emotional stakes of the story.

Chapter 7.

Political Context and Social Commentary

The Seed of the Sacred Fig is more than just a family drama; it is a searing reflection of the sociopolitical realities in modern-day Iran, particularly the oppressive nature of its authoritarian regime. Mohammad Rasoulof, the film's director, is an Iranian dissident whose work has continually challenged the theocratic rule and repression in his home country. In this film, Rasoulof delves deep into the ongoing struggle for freedom, justice, and personal autonomy in Iran, using the lens of a family torn apart by ideological conflict. Through its characters, visual metaphors, and narrative tension, the film serves as a potent commentary on the state of Iranian society, especially in relation to the treatment of women and the broader human rights abuses perpetuated by the regime.

Reflection of Real-Life Iranian Protests and the Oppression of Women:

At its core, The Seed of the Sacred Fig is a reflection of the real-life protests that have rocked Iran, particularly the anti-hijab demonstrations led by women in recent years. These protests are not just about the right to wear or not wear the hijab; they symbolize a broader demand for autonomy, freedom, and dignity in the face of systemic oppression. The film captures this reality through the character of Iman's daughters, Rezvan and Sana, who become increasingly vocal in their opposition to the regime's strict mandates on women's dress and behavior.

The oppression of women in Iran is a major theme in the film, and it is depicted with a raw, unflinching honesty. Rasoulof shows the brutal consequences of dissent, with female protesters being shot, beaten, and harassed by the authorities. The character of Najmeh, Iman's wife, represents the generation of Iranian women who have lived under the regime's harsh restrictions their entire lives but are now awakening to the possibility of change, spurred on by their daughters' courage. The film does not shy away from the horrors of state-sanctioned violence against women, which are depicted not only through the protests but also in the microcosm of Iman's home, where patriarchal authority mirrors the larger authoritarian structures of the state.

The real-life footage of protests, which Rasoulof weaves into the film, adds a layer of authenticity to the narrative, grounding it in the harsh realities faced by Iranian citizens. These moments of documentary-like footage are juxtaposed with the fictional story of Iman and his family, creating a seamless blend of the personal and the political. The images of women removing their hijabs in defiance of the law and being met with brutal force speak volumes about the regime's unwillingness to tolerate dissent. Rasoulof uses these moments to underscore the central conflict in the film: the clash between the desire for freedom and the oppressive forces that seek to maintain control.

Political Subtext: Critique of the Iranian Regime and Authoritarian Structures:

While The Seed of the Sacred Fig centers on the internal struggles of a single family, it is impossible to separate the personal from the political in Rasoulof's work. The film serves as a pointed critique of the Iranian regime, particularly its use of authoritarian structures to suppress dissent and maintain control over the populace. Iman, the protagonist, is emblematic of the moral corruption that often accompanies power in such regimes. As a newly promoted state investigator, Iman finds himself complicit in the very systems of repression that he once questioned. His gradual transformation from a decent man into a tool of the state reflects the broader dangers of authoritarianism, where individuals are often forced to sacrifice their morals and integrity in order to survive.

Iman's role as a state investigator, tasked with rubber-stamping death penalties without reviewing evidence, is a clear metaphor for the larger judicial system in Iran, which is widely criticized for its lack of transparency and fairness. The film highlights the ease with which the state can strip away an individual's humanity, turning them into a cog in the machine of repression. Iman's eventual embrace of the regime's propaganda and his authoritarian attitudes toward his daughters illustrate how authoritarianism seeps into every aspect of life, from the political to the personal.

The gun that Iman is given as part of his new role is a powerful symbol of state-sanctioned violence. It represents not only the physical threat posed by the regime but also the psychological control it exerts over its citizens. The gun becomes a source of tension in the household, reflecting the broader atmosphere of fear and paranoia that permeates Iranian society. Rasoulof's decision to make the gun a central element in the film's narrative speaks to the pervasive culture of violence and coercion that underpins authoritarian rule.

Through Iman's character arc, Rasoulof critiques not only the Iranian regime but also the individuals who enable its continued existence. Iman's moral decline is a stark reminder of the dangers of complacency and complicity in the face of injustice. The film suggests that in an authoritarian state, even those who start with good intentions can become agents of oppression if they are not vigilant in protecting their principles.

The Film's International Relevance: How It Speaks to Global Struggles for Freedom and Justice:

While The Seed of the Sacred Fig is deeply rooted in the specific political context of Iran, its themes of authoritarianism, patriarchal violence, and the struggle for personal freedom have universal resonance. The film speaks to global audiences by addressing issues that are not confined to Iran alone. Around the world, authoritarian regimes continue to use similar tactics of repression, whether through control of the judiciary, suppression of free speech, or violence against protestors. Rasoulof's film serves as a powerful reminder that the fight for freedom and justice is ongoing, not only in Iran but in many other parts of the world.

The film's exploration of the conflict between tradition and modernity, as seen through the generational divide between Iman and his daughters, resonates with audiences across different cultures. The daughters' desire for autonomy and their rejection of the oppressive traditions upheld by their father reflect a broader global trend, where younger generations are increasingly challenging the status quo and demanding change. The anti-hijab protests depicted in the film are just one example of this larger movement for freedom and equality, which can be seen in various forms across the world.

Rasoulof's film also has particular relevance in the current global context, where women's rights and bodily autonomy are being fiercely debated in many countries. The film's focus on the oppression of women in Iran echoes the struggles faced by women in other parts of the world, where patriarchal systems continue to limit their freedoms. The Seed of the Sacred Fig serves as a call to action, urging viewers to recognize the interconnectedness of these struggles and to stand in solidarity with those fighting for their rights.

Rasoulof's Personal Connection to the Story and His Real-Life Political Exile

Mohammad Rasoulof's personal experiences as a political dissident and filmmaker in exile are deeply woven into the fabric of The Seed of the Sacred Fig. Rasoulof has been a vocal critic of the Iranian regime for years, and his films have often been censored or banned in his home country. In 2017, he was sentenced to prison in Iran for his politically charged films, and he has since been living in exile, unable to return to his homeland without facing severe punishment.

Rasoulof's personal connection to the themes of repression and resistance is evident in the film's narrative. Like Iman, Rasoulof has had to grapple with the consequences of standing up to an authoritarian regime. His own experiences with censorship, surveillance, and the constant threat of imprisonment mirror the struggles faced by the characters in the film. Rasoulof's decision to include real-life protest footage further underscores his commitment to telling the truth about the situation in Iran, even at great personal risk.

In many ways, The Seed of the Sacred Fig can be seen as Rasoulof's own act of defiance against the Iranian regime. By making this film, Rasoulof is not only telling a story about one family's struggle for survival but also making a broader statement about the importance of resisting tyranny, no matter the cost. The film stands as a testament to Rasoulof's courage as a filmmaker and his unwavering dedication to shining a light on the injustices that plague his homeland.

Conclusion:

The Seed of the Sacred Fig is a politically charged film that offers a powerful critique of authoritarianism, patriarchal violence, and the oppression of women in Iran. Through its richly developed characters, symbolic use of visual metaphors, and incorporation of real-life protest footage, the film serves as both a reflection of the current sociopolitical climate in Iran and a broader commentary on the global struggle for freedom and justice. Rasoulof's personal connection to the story, rooted in his own experiences as a political dissident, adds depth and authenticity to the narrative, making it not just a film but a bold statement of resistance against tyranny.

Chapter 8.

Pacing and Narrative Structure

In The Seed of the Sacred Fig, Mohammad Rasoulof masterfully blends political drama with suspense, creating a dynamic narrative structure that mirrors the escalating tension within both the characters' lives and the larger political context of Iran. The pacing of the film, which shifts from slow-building introspection to a high-stakes thriller, reflects the increasing pressures faced by the characters as they are drawn deeper into the web of authoritarian control and personal conflict. This chapter delves into the careful construction of the film's pacing and narrative structure, exploring how Rasoulof uses these elements to enhance the thematic and emotional depth of the story.

The Shift in Tone from Political Drama to Suspense Thriller:

At the outset, The Seed of the Sacred Fig presents itself as a relatively slow-moving political drama, focusing on the domestic life of Iman, an ambitious lawyer promoted to state investigator, and his family. The opening scenes are characterized by a sense of routine and normalcy, albeit tinged with the underlying tension that accompanies life under an authoritarian regime. The pacing is deliberate, allowing viewers to immerse themselves in the family's daily interactions, the subtleties of their relationships, and the growing ideological divide between Iman and his daughters, Rezvan and Sana. The political climate in Iran marked by anti-hijab protests and increasing state repression hovers in the background, influencing the characters' choices but not yet overtaking the narrative.

However, as the film progresses, there is a noticeable shift in tone. What begins as a domestic political drama gradually transforms into a suspense-filled thriller. This shift is marked by key narrative events, such as Iman's discovery that his new role requires him to rubber-stamp death penalty judgments without reviewing evidence, and his eventual realization that he is being watched and manipulated by the very system he once trusted. The introduction of the gun into the household an object that becomes a symbol of both state-sanctioned violence and familial discord further heightens the sense of danger. As the political tensions outside the home escalate, so too does the psychological and emotional tension within the family.

Rasoulof's decision to shift the film's tone from political drama to suspense thriller mirrors the increasing unpredictability of life in an authoritarian state. As Iman becomes more deeply entrenched in his role as a state investigator, he finds himself trapped in a system that demands absolute loyalty and punishes even the slightest hint of dissent. The slow build-up of political and personal tension gives way to moments of sudden violence and paranoia, reflecting the unpredictable nature of life under a repressive regime. This shift in tone keeps viewers on edge, as the stakes become higher with each passing scene.

The Build-Up of Tension and How the Film Escalates:

The tension in The Seed of the Sacred Fig is built gradually, with Rasoulof employing a careful balance of character development, dialogue, and visual symbolism to convey the growing sense of unease. Early in the film, the tension is subtle, manifesting primarily in the strained conversations between Iman and his daughters, who challenge his increasingly authoritarian views. The conflict between Iman's desire to maintain order and his daughters' rebellious spirit is emblematic of the larger societal conflict between the Iranian regime and its people. These early moments of tension are quiet but palpable, setting the stage for the film's eventual escalation.

As the political situation outside the home intensifies with anti-hijab protests gaining momentum and the state responding with brutal crackdowns the tension within the family also escalates. Rasoulof masterfully uses this parallel structure to heighten the stakes, showing how the political and the personal are inextricably linked. The arrival of the gun in the household serves as a turning point, symbolizing the increasing militarization of everyday life and the way in which violence, both state-sanctioned and personal, infiltrates the most intimate spaces.

The film's pacing becomes more urgent as Iman's world begins to unravel. His suspicion that one of his family members has taken the gun leads to a series of confrontations that escalate both emotionally and physically. Rasoulof's use of suspenseful pacing here is particularly effective; each scene builds upon the last, with the tension mounting as Iman's paranoia grows. The audience, like Iman, is left to question the motivations of each character, unsure of who can be trusted and what will happen next.

The use of real-life protest footage interspersed throughout the film adds to the sense of urgency and escalation. These moments of documentary-like realism serve as reminders of the stakes outside the home, grounding the narrative in the real-world political struggle that the characters are a part of. The juxtaposition of these protest scenes with the increasingly volatile dynamics within the family creates a powerful sense of inevitability, as both the political and personal conflicts hurtle toward a dramatic conclusion.

Handling of Character Development and Thematic Exploration within the Structure:

One of the strengths of The Seed of the Sacred Fig is its ability to balance character development with thematic exploration, all within the context of its escalating narrative structure. Rasoulof takes care to develop each of the main characters in a way that feels organic and deeply connected to the film's broader political themes. Iman's transformation from a principled lawyer to a morally compromised state investigator is central to the film's exploration of how authoritarian regimes corrupt individuals from within. His growing paranoia and authoritarianism are mirrored in his increasingly controlling behavior toward his family, particularly his daughters, who represent the younger generation's desire for freedom and change.

Rezvan and Sana, as representatives of this younger generation, undergo their own development over the course of the film. Initially portrayed as somewhat passive in the face of their father's authority, they gradually become more outspoken, challenging both Iman's views and the broader patriarchal structures that oppress them. Their involvement in helping a young anti-hijab protester who has been shot by the police serves as a pivotal moment in their development, signaling their willingness to take risks and stand up for what they believe in, even at great personal cost.

Najmeh, Iman's wife, also undergoes significant development, though hers is more internalized. As the family's tensions rise, Najmeh is caught between her loyalty to her husband and her desire to protect her daughters from the authoritarian forces that have taken hold of their lives. Her quiet resilience and eventual defiance are key to the film's thematic exploration of women's resistance to both familial and societal oppression.

Thematically, Rasoulof uses the characters' development to explore broader issues such as the conflict between tradition and modernity, the corrupting influence of power, and the struggle for personal and political autonomy. Each character's arc is carefully woven into the larger narrative structure, ensuring that their personal journeys feel integral to the film's exploration of these complex themes.

How the Third Act Intensifies the Emotional and Political Stakes:

The third act of The Seed of the Sacred Fig is where the film's pacing reaches its peak, with both the emotional and political stakes intensifying to a dramatic crescendo. The loss of the gun becomes a central plot point, driving the final act's suspense and pushing the characters to their breaking points. Iman's growing paranoia and frustration lead to increasingly volatile confrontations with his family, as he becomes convinced that one of them has taken the gun and is lying to him. This sense of betrayal, both personal and ideological, adds a layer of emotional complexity to the final act, as Iman's world crumbles around him.

Politically, the third act also escalates the stakes. The protests outside the home reach a fever pitch, with the regime responding with brutal violence. The real-life footage of these protests, combined with the escalating tension within the household, creates a powerful sense of urgency. Rasoulof's use of pacing here is particularly effective, as the film's slow build-up gives way to a rapid, almost chaotic series of events that mirror the chaos unfolding in the streets.

The film's climax, which involves a shocking act of violence, brings the emotional and political stakes to a head. Rasoulof ensures that this moment is not just a narrative payoff but also a thematic one, encapsulating the film's exploration of the corrosive effects of authoritarianism on both the individual and the family. The final moments of the film, in which the consequences of this violence are revealed, leave the audience with a sense of both devastation and clarity, as the full weight of the film's themes comes crashing down.

Conclusion:

In The Seed of the Sacred Fig, Mohammad Rasoulof masterfully uses pacing and narrative structure to build tension and explore complex themes. The film's shift from political drama to suspense thriller mirrors the escalating stakes in both the characters' lives and the larger political context of Iran. Through careful character development and thematic exploration, Rasoulof ensures that the film's pacing serves not only to create suspense but also to deepen the audience's understanding of the personal and political struggles at its core. The third act's intense emotional and political climax brings the film's themes to a powerful and resonant conclusion, leaving a lasting impact on the viewer.

Chapter 9.

Criticism and Flaws

While The Seed of the Sacred Fig is a powerful and compelling film that tackles important themes of authoritarianism, patriarchal violence, and personal resistance, it is not without its flaws. As with any ambitious piece of cinema, there are aspects of the film's plot development, character arcs, and stylistic choices that may leave some viewers feeling unsatisfied or questioning the coherence of the narrative. In this chapter, we will explore some of the potential shortcomings in the film, including ambiguities in the plot, missed opportunities for character development, and the tension between its realist and abstract elements.

Flaws in Plot Development and Character Arcs:

One of the criticisms that can be leveled against The Seed of the Sacred Fig is the inconsistency in the development of certain characters, particularly Iman, the film's central figure. While Iman's journey from a principled lawyer to a morally compromised state investigator is at the heart of the narrative, there are moments where his transformation feels rushed or underexplored. Early in the film, Iman is portrayed as a man of conscience, someone who is uncomfortable with the authoritarian demands of his new role. However, his shift toward authoritarianism and paranoia occurs so quickly that it can feel jarring. The film doesn't fully explore the internal struggle that would likely accompany such a radical transformation, leaving the audience to fill in the gaps.

Iman's increasing authoritarianism toward his family, particularly his daughters, is central to the film's exploration of patriarchal violence, but there are moments where his motivations feel underdeveloped. His sudden coldness and paranoia regarding his daughters' political views and actions, while believable in the context of the film's broader themes, could have been more carefully unpacked. The film presents Iman as a man deeply conflicted between his role as a father and his loyalty to the regime, but the internal conflict that would likely accompany this shift is not always fully explored. As a result, some viewers may find Iman's character arc incomplete or lacking in psychological depth.

Similarly, while the daughters, Rezvan and Sana, serve as important symbols of the younger generation's resistance to the regime's patriarchal and authoritarian structures, their individual personalities and motivations are not as fully fleshed out as they could be. The film positions them as ideological foils to their father, representing the desire for freedom and change, but it doesn't delve deeply into their personal experiences or struggles. Their involvement in helping the young anti-hijab protester is a pivotal moment in the plot, but beyond this act of resistance, we don't learn much about their inner lives or what drives them. This lack of character development leaves them feeling more like symbols than fully realized individuals, which detracts from the emotional impact of the story.

Najmeh, Iman's wife, also suffers from underdevelopment. While her quiet resilience and eventual defiance are key to the film's thematic exploration of women's resistance, her character arc feels somewhat sidelined. Her role as a mediator between Iman and their daughters is clear, but her personal feelings about the political and familial conflict remain largely unexplored. As a result, Najmeh's emotional journey feels incomplete, and her eventual defiance, while powerful, lacks the necessary buildup to make it feel fully earned.

Ambiguities and Missed Opportunities:

One of the most striking aspects of The Seed of the Sacred Fig is its use of ambiguity, both in terms of plot and character motivations. While ambiguity can be a powerful narrative tool, allowing for multiple interpretations and encouraging viewers to engage more deeply with the film, it can also create a sense of frustration if not handled carefully. In Rasoulof's film, there are moments where the ambiguity feels more like a missed opportunity than a deliberate artistic choice.

For example, the mystery surrounding the missing gun a central plot device introduces a level of suspense and paranoia that drives the narrative forward. However, the film's resolution of this subplot feels anticlimactic. The question of who took the gun and why is never fully resolved, leaving the audience with more questions than answers. While this ambiguity may be intended to reflect the uncertainty and chaos of life under authoritarian rule, it also feels like a missed opportunity to explore the psychological and emotional consequences of Iman's growing paranoia. By leaving this key plot point unresolved, the film risks undermining the tension it worked so hard to build.

Additionally, the film's exploration of the broader political conflict in Iran, particularly the anti-hijab protests, is somewhat underdeveloped. While the film includes real-life footage of these protests, which adds a sense of urgency and realism to the narrative, it doesn't fully explore the motivations of the protestors or the regime's response. The protests serve as a backdrop to the family's personal conflict, but they are not integrated into the narrative in a meaningful way. This lack of integration creates a disconnect between the personal and political dimensions of the film, making the broader societal struggle feel somewhat distant from the characters' immediate experiences.

There is also a sense that the film could have delved deeper into the psychological consequences of living under authoritarian rule. While we see Iman's increasing paranoia and authoritarianism, the film doesn't fully explore the impact of this environment on the rest of the family. Rezvan and

Sana's defiance is clear, but we don't get a sense of the fear or anxiety they might feel as they navigate life in a repressive society. Similarly, Najmeh's internal conflict is only hinted at, leaving the audience to wonder how she truly feels about her husband's transformation and the political situation around her.

Realist Elements versus Abstract Moments:

One of the most distinctive features of The Seed of the Sacred Fig is its blending of realist and abstract elements. Rasoulof uses a realist approach to depict the everyday lives of the characters, grounding the film in the harsh realities of life under an authoritarian regime. The use of real-life protest footage, for example, adds a documentary-like quality to the film, reminding the audience that the events depicted are not purely fictional but are rooted in the real-world struggles of the Iranian people.

However, the film also includes more abstract, symbolic moments, particularly in its use of the gun as a metaphor for both state-sanctioned violence and personal power. While these abstract elements add depth to the narrative, there is a potential disconnect between the film's realist and symbolic layers. Some viewers may find that the shift between these two modes of storytelling feels disjointed, creating a sense of narrative inconsistency.

For example, the gun, which plays such a central role in the film's symbolism, is introduced in a relatively casual manner, with little explanation as to why Iman would be so careless with such a dangerous object. This lack of realism in the handling of the gun creates a disconnect between the film's otherwise grounded depiction of life under authoritarian rule. Similarly, the film's climax, which involves a sudden act of violence, feels more like a symbolic resolution to the film's thematic concerns than a realistic conclusion to the characters' personal conflict. While this abstract approach may resonate with some viewers, others may find it jarring or unsatisfying, particularly if they were expecting a more grounded, realist narrative.

Conclusion:

The Seed of the Sacred Fig is an ambitious and important film that tackles difficult themes with courage and urgency. However, it is not without its flaws. The inconsistencies in character development, the unresolved plot points, and the tension between the film's realist and abstract elements may leave some viewers feeling unsatisfied. While Rasoulof's use of ambiguity adds depth to the narrative, there are moments where it feels more like a missed opportunity than a deliberate artistic choice. Despite these flaws, the film's strengths—its exploration of authoritarianism, patriarchal violence, and personal resistance—make it a significant contribution to contemporary Iranian cinema.

Chapter 10.

Conclusion

In The Seed of the Sacred Fig, Mohammad Rasoulof presents a bold and intricate exploration of life under an authoritarian regime, where patriarchal values, theocracy, and political repression converge in an intensely personal narrative. The film grapples with some of the most pressing socio-political issues in Iran today—specifically the oppression of women and the increasing authoritarian grip of the state while telling the story of one family's descent into paranoia, distrust, and confrontation. In this final chapter, we offer a comprehensive assessment of the film, evaluating its performances, direction, thematic execution, and its place in both Iranian and world cinema. We also consider the broader cultural and political implications of Rasoulof's brave cinematic work.

Overall Assessment of the Film:

The Seed of the Sacred Fig is an ambitious, layered film that seeks to reflect the complex realities of life in Iran through the lens of personal and familial conflict. The narrative draws upon Rasoulof's personal experiences with repression and censorship, and the film as a whole acts as a pointed critique of authoritarianism. The central character, Iman, undergoes a transformation that mirrors the societal pressures that many individuals in positions of power face in an authoritarian state. Rasoulof uses this transformation to highlight the corrosive effects of the regime not just on political dissidents, but also on those who are ostensibly part of the system.

The film's storyline unfolds gradually, taking its time to establish the dynamics within Iman's family and their fraught relationship with the political situation in Iran. As Iman's professional role demands increasing moral compromises, his home life begins to disintegrate. The eventual escalation of tension, culminating in an act of violence, serves as a powerful metaphor for the way authoritarian systems breed violence within society at large. By grounding this societal critique in the intimate setting of a family home, Rasoulof makes the political personal, showing how the oppressive structures of the state infiltrate even the most private aspects of life.

Though the film's pacing may seem slow to some, its measured approach allows for a deep exploration of the characters and themes. Rasoulof makes effective use of subtlety and suggestion, leaving much of the narrative's tension to simmer beneath the surface before finally erupting. While the climax might seem abrupt to some viewers, it ultimately serves the film's broader commentary on violence and repression both inevitable outcomes of the toxic environment the characters inhabit.

Evaluation of the Performances, Direction, and Thematic Execution:

One of the film's greatest strengths is the performances of its lead actors, particularly Missagh Zareh as Iman and Soheila Golestani as Najmeh. Zareh delivers a nuanced portrayal of a man caught between his moral convictions and the demands of his new role as a state investigator. His gradual shift from a principled, introspective individual to an authoritarian enforcer is handled with subtlety, showing how internal conflict and external pressures can erode a person's integrity. Zareh's ability to convey Iman's mounting paranoia and frustration adds emotional weight to the film's examination of power and corruption.

Soheila Golestani, as Iman's wife Najmeh, offers a quieter but equally compelling performance. Her portrayal of a woman struggling to maintain her family's unity in the face of growing political and domestic conflict speaks to the broader struggles of women in Iran, who must navigate both societal expectations and personal aspirations. Golestani's understated performance provides a counterpoint to Iman's increasingly volatile behavior, representing resilience in the face of oppression. Her character's eventual defiance, though subtle, resonates with the film's overarching message about resistance.

The daughters, Rezvan and Sana, played by Setareh Malek and Mahsa Rostami, embody the generational divide that often exists in authoritarian societies. Their roles, while not as deeply developed as those of Iman and Najmeh, serve to highlight the clash between traditional values and the desire for change. Their political engagement and opposition to their father's views add a layer of complexity to the family dynamic, with their actions reflecting the broader youth-led protest movements in Iran. While their characters might have benefited from more in-depth exploration, they still serve as essential components in the film's depiction of societal conflict.

Rasoulof's direction is marked by a deliberate, calculated approach to storytelling. His use of framing and composition enhances the sense of entrapment that pervades the film. The camera often lingers on characters in confined spaces whether it be the family's home or Iman's office visually reinforcing the idea that they are all trapped by the oppressive political and social structures around them. This visual claustrophobia serves as a metaphor for the characters' emotional and psychological states, underscoring the film's central themes.

Rasoulof's thematic execution is both ambitious and brave. He uses Iman's personal story to explore broader issues of patriarchal violence, the moral compromises required by authoritarian systems, and the conflict between tradition and modernity. The gun, which plays a central role in the film, serves as a potent symbol of both state-sanctioned violence and personal power. The film's gradual shift from a political drama to a suspenseful, almost thriller-like narrative reflects the increasing tension in Iranian society, where public protest and private resistance often give way to violent repression.

The Film's Significance within Iranian Cinema and World Cinema:

The Seed of the Sacred Fig stands out as an important film within the context of Iranian cinema. Mohammad Rasoulof, already known for his previous works that critique the Iranian regime, continues to push boundaries with this film. His willingness to address such politically sensitive topics, particularly the treatment of women and the authoritarian grip of the state, marks him as one of the most courageous filmmakers working in Iran today. Given that Rasoulof himself has faced imprisonment and censorship for his work, the film's very existence is a testament to the director's resilience and commitment to using cinema as a form of political resistance.

In the broader context of world cinema, The Seed of the Sacred Fig holds its own as a film that speaks to universal themes of power, repression, and resistance. While the story is firmly rooted in the political landscape of Iran, its themes resonate far beyond the country's borders. The film's exploration of patriarchal violence, authoritarianism, and the tension between personal and political identities is relevant to societies around the world that are grappling with similar issues. As a result, the film's appeal is not limited to those familiar with Iranian politics but extends to anyone interested in the global struggle for freedom and justice.

Final Thoughts on Its Cultural Relevance and Political Bravery:

Culturally, The Seed of the Sacred Fig is significant not only for its portrayal of life in contemporary Iran but also for its broader commentary on the human cost of authoritarianism. By focusing on the intimate struggles of one family, Rasoulof is able to explore the ways in which political repression seeps into the most private aspects of life. The film highlights the ways in which patriarchal and authoritarian systems rely on fear and control, not just at the societal level but within families as well. This cultural relevance is underscored by the film's use of real-life protest footage, which serves as a powerful reminder of the ongoing struggles for freedom in Iran and beyond.

Politically, Rasoulof's film is an act of defiance. His choice to address such sensitive topics, particularly the anti-hijab protests and the regime's treatment of women, speaks to his bravery as a filmmaker. In a country where censorship is rampant and political dissent is often met with severe consequences, Rasoulof's willingness to critique the regime through his art is nothing short of courageous. By creating a film that challenges the status quo and gives voice to those who are often silenced, Rasoulof continues to play a crucial role in the ongoing fight for freedom of expression in Iran.

In conclusion, The Seed of the Sacred Fig is a powerful, thought-provoking film that succeeds in addressing complex political and social issues while also telling a compelling personal story. Despite its flaws, the film's strengths its performances, direction, and thematic depth make it an important work within both Iranian and world cinema. Rasoulof's bold storytelling and political bravery ensure that the film will remain culturally and politically relevant for years to come, serving as a testament to the power of cinema as a tool for resistance and social change.

Manufactured by Amazon.ca
Bolton, ON